Baby Shower Guest Book

Estimated Due Date

. . . .

Actual Delivery Date

. . . .

Guest Name

....

Address and Email

....

....

....

Best Advice for Parents

....

....

....

Special Message to Baby

....

....

....

My Predictions

Date of Birth _____ Time of Birth _____ Weight _____

Most Resemblance _____ I Hope The Baby Gets Moms _____

I Hope The Baby Gets Dads _____

Guest Name

Address and Email

....

....

....

....

Best Advice for Parents

....

....

....

Special Message to Baby

....

....

....

My Predictions

Date of Birth _____ Time of Birth_____ Weight_____

Most Resemblance _____ I Hope The Baby Gets Moms _____

I Hope The Baby Gets Dads _____

Guest Name

Address and Email

....

....

....

....

Best Advice for Parents

....

....

....

Special Message to Baby

....

....

....

My Predictions

Date of Birth _____ Time of Birth_____ Weight_____

Most Resemblance _____ I Hope The Baby Gets Moms _____

I Hope The Baby Gets Dads _____

Guest Name

Address and Email

....

....

....

....

Best Advice for Parents

....

....

....

Special Message to Baby

....

....

....

My Predictions

Date of Birth _____ Time of Birth_____ Weight_____

Most Resemblance _____ I Hope The Baby Gets Moms _____

I Hope The Baby Gets Dads _____

Happy Memories

Happy Memories

Guest Name

Address and Email

....

....

....

....

Best Advice for Parents

....

....

....

Special Message to Baby

....

....

....

My Predictions

Date of Birth _____ Time of Birth _____ Weight _____

Most Resemblance _____ I Hope The Baby Gets Moms _____

I Hope The Baby Gets Dads _____

Guest Name

Address and Email

....

....

....

Best Advice for Parents

....

....

....

Special Message to Baby

....

....

....

My Predictions

Date of Birth _____ Time of Birth_____ Weight_____

Most Resemblance _____ I Hope The Baby Gets Moms _____

I Hope The Baby Gets Dads _____

Guest Name

Address and Email

....

....

....

....

Best Advice for Parents

....

....

....

Special Message to Baby

....

....

....

My Predictions

Date of Birth _____ Time of Birth _____ Weight _____

Most Resemblance _____ I Hope The Baby Gets Moms _____

I Hope The Baby Gets Dads _____

Guest Name

Address and Email

....

....

....

Best Advice for Parents

....

....

....

Special Message to Baby

....

....

....

My Predictions

Date of Birth _____ Time of Birth_____ Weight_____

Most Resemblance _____ I Hope The Baby Gets Moms _____

I Hope The Baby Gets Dads _____

Happy Memories

Happy Memories

Guest Name

Address and Email

....

....

....

....

Best Advice for Parents

....

....

....

Special Message to Baby

....

....

....

My Predictions

Date of Birth .... Time of Birth .... Weight ....

Most Resemblance .... I Hope The Baby Gets Moms ....

I Hope The Baby Gets Dads ....

Guest Name

Address and Email

....

....

....

....

Best Advice for Parents

....

....

....

Special Message to Baby

....

....

....

My Predictions

Date of Birth .... Time of Birth........................ Weight........................

Most Resemblance .... I Hope The Baby Gets Moms ....

I Hope The Baby Gets Dads ....

Guest Name

Address and Email

....

....

....

....

Best Advice for Parents

....

....

....

Special Message to Baby

....

....

....

My Predictions

Date of Birth _____ Time of Birth _____ Weight _____

Most Resemblance _____ I Hope The Baby Gets Moms _____

I Hope The Baby Gets Dads _____

Guest Name

Address and Email

....

....

....

....

....

Best Advice for Parents

....

....

....

Special Message to Baby

....

....

....

My Predictions

Date of Birth _____ Time of Birth_____ Weight_____

Most Resemblance _____ I Hope The Baby Gets Moms _____

I Hope The Baby Gets Dads _____

Happy Memories

Happy Memories

Guest Name

Address and Email

....

....

....

....

Best Advice for Parents

....

....

....

Special Message to Baby

....

....

....

My Predictions

Date of Birth _____ Time of Birth_____ Weight_____

Most Resemblance _____ I Hope The Baby Gets Moms _____

I Hope The Baby Gets Dads _____

Guest Name

Address and Email

....

....

....

....

Best Advice for Parents

....

....

....

Special Message to Baby

....

....

....

My Predictions

Date of Birth _____ Time of Birth_____ Weight_____

Most Resemblance _____ I Hope The Baby Gets Moms _____

I Hope The Baby Gets Dads _____

Guest Name

Address and Email

....

....

....

....

Best Advice for Parents

....

....

....

Special Message to Baby

....

....

....

My Predictions

Date of Birth .... Time of Birth .... Weight ....

Most Resemblance .... I Hope The Baby Gets Moms ....

I Hope The Baby Gets Dads ....

Guest Name

Address and Email

....

....

....

....

Best Advice for Parents

....

....

....

Special Message to Baby

....

....

....

My Predictions

Date of Birth .... Time of Birth................................ Weight................................

Most Resemblance .... I Hope The Baby Gets Moms ....

I Hope The Baby Gets Dads ....

Happy Memories

Happy Memories

Guest Name

Address and Email

....

....

....

....

Best Advice for Parents

....

....

....

Special Message to Baby

....

....

....

My Predictions

Date of Birth _____ Time of Birth_____ Weight_____

Most Resemblance _____ I Hope The Baby Gets Moms _____

I Hope The Baby Gets Dads _____

Guest Name

Address and Email

....

....

....

....

Best Advice for Parents

....

....

....

Special Message to Baby

....

....

....

My Predictions

Date of Birth _____ Time of Birth _____ Weight_____

Most Resemblance _____ I Hope The Baby Gets Moms _____

I Hope The Baby Gets Dads _____

Guest Name

....

Address and Email

....

....

....

Best Advice for Parents

....

....

....

Special Message to Baby

....

....

....

My Predictions

Date of Birth _____ Time of Birth_____ Weight_____

Most Resemblance _____ I Hope The Baby Gets Moms _____

I Hope The Baby Gets Dads _____

Guest Name

Address and Email

....

....

....

Best Advice for Parents

....

....

....

Special Message to Baby

....

....

....

My Predictions

Date of Birth _____ Time of Birth_____ Weight_____

Most Resemblance _____ I Hope The Baby Gets Moms _____

I Hope The Baby Gets Dads _____

Happy Memories

Happy Memories

Guest Name

Address and Email

....

....

....

....

Best Advice for Parents

....

....

....

Special Message to Baby

....

....

....

My Predictions

Date of Birth .... Time of Birth .... Weight ....

Most Resemblance .... I Hope The Baby Gets Moms ....

I Hope The Baby Gets Dads ....

Guest Name

Address and Email

....

....

....

Best Advice for Parents

....

....

....

Special Message to Baby

....

....

....

My Predictions

Date of Birth .... Time of Birth........................ Weight........................

Most Resemblance .... I Hope The Baby Gets Moms ....

I Hope The Baby Gets Dads ....

Guest Name

Address and Email

....

....

....

....

Best Advice for Parents

....

....

....

Special Message to Baby

....

....

....

My Predictions

Date of Birth .... Time of Birth........................ Weight........................

Most Resemblance .... I Hope The Baby Gets Moms ....

I Hope The Baby Gets Dads ....

Guest Name

Address and Email

....

....

....

....

Best Advice for Parents

....

....

....

Special Message to Baby

....

....

....

My Predictions

Date of Birth .... Time of Birth............................ Weight............................

Most Resemblance .... I Hope The Baby Gets Moms ....

I Hope The Baby Gets Dads ....

Happy Memories

Happy Memories

Guest Name

Address and Email

....

....

....

....

Best Advice for Parents

....

....

....

Special Message to Baby

....

....

....

My Predictions

Date of Birth .... Time of Birth.......................... Weight...........................

Most Resemblance .... I Hope The Baby Gets Moms ....

I Hope The Baby Gets Dads ....

Guest Name

....

Address and Email

....
....
....

Best Advice for Parents

....
....
....

Special Message to Baby

....
....
....

My Predictions

Date of Birth .... Time of Birth........................ Weight........................

Most Resemblance .... I Hope The Baby Gets Moms ....

I Hope The Baby Gets Dads ....

Guest Name

Address and Email

....

....

....

....

Best Advice for Parents

....

....

....

Special Message to Baby

....

....

....

My Predictions

Date of Birth _____ Time of Birth_____ Weight_____

Most Resemblance _____ I Hope The Baby Gets Moms _____

I Hope The Baby Gets Dads _____

Guest Name

Address and Email

....

....

....

Best Advice for Parents

....

....

....

Special Message to Baby

....

....

....

My Predictions

Date of Birth _____ Time of Birth_____ Weight_____

Most Resemblance _____ I Hope The Baby Gets Moms _____

I Hope The Baby Gets Dads _____

Happy Memories

Happy Memories

Guest Name

Address and Email

....

....

....

....

Best Advice for Parents

....

....

....

Special Message to Baby

....

....

....

My Predictions

Date of Birth .... Time of Birth .... Weight ....

Most Resemblance .... I Hope The Baby Gets Moms ....

I Hope The Baby Gets Dads ....

Guest Name

Address and Email

....

....

....

....

Best Advice for Parents

....

....

....

Special Message to Baby

....

....

....

My Predictions

Date of Birth _____ Time of Birth_____ Weight_____

Most Resemblance _____ I Hope The Baby Gets Moms _____

I Hope The Baby Gets Dads _____

Guest Name

....

Address and Email

....

....

....

Best Advice for Parents

....

....

....

Special Message to Baby

....

....

....

My Predictions

Date of Birth .... Time of Birth .... Weight ....

Most Resemblance .... I Hope The Baby Gets Moms ....

I Hope The Baby Gets Dads ....

Guest Name

Address and Email

....

....

....

....

Best Advice for Parents

....

....

....

Special Message to Baby

....

....

....

My Predictions

Date of Birth .... Time of Birth .... Weight ....

Most Resemblance .... I Hope The Baby Gets Moms ....

I Hope The Baby Gets Dads ....

Happy Memories

Happy Memories

Guest Name

Address and Email

....

....

....

....

Best Advice for Parents

....

....

....

Special Message to Baby

....

....

....

My Predictions

Date of Birth .... Time of Birth........................... Weight...........................

Most Resemblance .... I Hope The Baby Gets Moms ....

I Hope The Baby Gets Dads ....

Guest Name

Address and Email

....
                                                       ....
                                                       ....

Best Advice for Parents

....

....

....

Special Message to Baby

....

....

....

My Predictions

Date of Birth .... Time of Birth.. Weight...........................

Most Resemblance .... I Hope The Baby Gets Moms ....

I Hope The Baby Gets Dads ....

Guest Name

Address and Email

....

....

....

....

Best Advice for Parents

....

....

....

Special Message to Baby

....

....

....

My Predictions

Date of Birth _____ Time of Birth _____ Weight_____

Most Resemblance _____ I Hope The Baby Gets Moms _____

I Hope The Baby Gets Dads _____

Guest Name

Address and Email

....

....

....

Best Advice for Parents

....

....

....

Special Message to Baby

....

....

....

My Predictions

Date of Birth _____ Time of Birth_____ Weight_____

Most Resemblance _____ I Hope The Baby Gets Moms _____

I Hope The Baby Gets Dads _____

Happy Memories

Happy Memories

Guest Name

Address and Email

....

....

....

....

Best Advice for Parents

....

....

....

Special Message to Baby

....

....

....

My Predictions

Date of Birth _____ Time of Birth _____ Weight _____

Most Resemblance _____ I Hope The Baby Gets Moms _____

I Hope The Baby Gets Dads _____

Guest Name

Address and Email

....

....

....

Best Advice for Parents

....

....

....

Special Message to Baby

....

....

....

My Predictions

Date of Birth .... Time of Birth.. Weight..

Most Resemblance .... I Hope The Baby Gets Moms ....

I Hope The Baby Gets Dads ....

Guest Name

Address and Email

....

....

....

....

Best Advice for Parents

....

....

....

Special Message to Baby

....

....

....

My Predictions

Date of Birth .... Time of Birth........................ Weight........................

Most Resemblance .... I Hope The Baby Gets Moms ....

I Hope The Baby Gets Dads ....

Guest Name

Address and Email

....

....

....

Best Advice for Parents

....

....

....

Special Message to Baby

....

....

....

My Predictions

Date of Birth .... Time of Birth........................... Weight...........................

Most Resemblance .... I Hope The Baby Gets Moms ....

I Hope The Baby Gets Dads ....

Happy Memories

Happy Memories

Guest Name

....

Address and Email

....

....

....

Best Advice for Parents

....

....

....

Special Message to Baby

....

....

....

My Predictions

Date of Birth _____ Time of Birth_____ Weight_____

Most Resemblance _____ I Hope The Baby Gets Moms _____

I Hope The Baby Gets Dads _____

Guest Name

Address and Email

....

....

....

....

Best Advice for Parents

....

....

....

Special Message to Baby

....

....

....

My Predictions

Date of Birth .... Time of Birth........................... Weight...........................

Most Resemblance .... I Hope The Baby Gets Moms ....

I Hope The Baby Gets Dads ....

Guest Name

Address and Email

....

....

....

Best Advice for Parents

....

....

....

Special Message to Baby

....

....

....

My Predictions

Date of Birth _____ Time of Birth_____ Weight_____

Most Resemblance _____ I Hope The Baby Gets Moms _____

I Hope The Baby Gets Dads _____

Guest Name

Address and Email

....

....

....

....

Best Advice for Parents

....

....

....

Special Message to Baby

....

....

....

My Predictions

Date of Birth .... Time of Birth........................... Weight...........................

Most Resemblance .... I Hope The Baby Gets Moms ....

I Hope The Baby Gets Dads ....

Happy Memories

Happy Memories

Guest Name

Address and Email

....

....

....

....

Best Advice for Parents

....

....

....

Special Message to Baby

....

....

....

My Predictions

Date of Birth .... Time of Birth .... Weight ....

Most Resemblance .... I Hope The Baby Gets Moms ....

I Hope The Baby Gets Dads ....

Guest Name

Address and Email

....

....

....

Best Advice for Parents

....

....

....

Special Message to Baby

....

....

....

My Predictions

Date of Birth .... Time of Birth............................... Weight...............................

Most Resemblance .... I Hope The Baby Gets Moms ....

I Hope The Baby Gets Dads ....

Guest Name

Address and Email

....

....

Best Advice for Parents

....

....

....

Special Message to Baby

....

....

....

My Predictions

Date of Birth .... Time of Birth................... Weight....................

Most Resemblance .... I Hope The Baby Gets Moms ....

I Hope The Baby Gets Dads ....

Guest Name

Address and Email

....

....

....

....

Best Advice for Parents

....

....

....

Special Message to Baby

....

....

....

My Predictions

Date of Birth .... Time of Birth .... Weight ....

Most Resemblance .... I Hope The Baby Gets Moms ....

I Hope The Baby Gets Dads ....

Happy Memories

Happy Memories

Guest Name

Address and Email

....

....

....

....

....

Best Advice for Parents

....

....

....

Special Message to Baby

....

....

....

My Predictions

Date of Birth .... Time of Birth .... Weight ....

Most Resemblance .... I Hope The Baby Gets Moms ....

I Hope The Baby Gets Dads ....

Guest Name

Address and Email

....

....

....

Best Advice for Parents

....

....

....

Special Message to Baby

....

....

....

My Predictions

Date of Birth .... Time of Birth........................ Weight........................

Most Resemblance .... I Hope The Baby Gets Moms ....

I Hope The Baby Gets Dads ....

Guest Name

Address and Email

....

....

....

....

Best Advice for Parents

....

....

....

Special Message to Baby

....

....

....

My Predictions

Date of Birth .... Time of Birth .... Weight ....

Most Resemblance .... I Hope The Baby Gets Moms ....

I Hope The Baby Gets Dads ....

Guest Name

Address and Email

....

....

....

Best Advice for Parents

....

....

....

Special Message to Baby

....

....

....

My Predictions

Date of Birth .... Time of Birth........................ Weight........................

Most Resemblance .... I Hope The Baby Gets Moms ....

I Hope The Baby Gets Dads ....

Happy Memories

Happy Memories

Guest Name

Address and Email

....

....

....

Best Advice for Parents

....

....

....

Special Message to Baby

....

....

....

My Predictions

Date of Birth .... Time of Birth .... Weight ....

Most Resemblance .... I Hope The Baby Gets Moms ....

I Hope The Baby Gets Dads ....

Guest Name

Address and Email

....

....

....

Best Advice for Parents

....

....

....

Special Message to Baby

....

....

....

My Predictions

Date of Birth .... Time of Birth........................ Weight........................

Most Resemblance .... I Hope The Baby Gets Moms ....

I Hope The Baby Gets Dads ....

Guest Name

Address and Email

....

....

....

....

Best Advice for Parents

....

....

....

Special Message to Baby

....

....

....

My Predictions

Date of Birth _____ Time of Birth_____ Weight_____

Most Resemblance _____ I Hope The Baby Gets Moms _____

I Hope The Baby Gets Dads _____

Guest Name

Address and Email

....

....

....

Best Advice for Parents

....

....

....

Special Message to Baby

....

....

....

My Predictions

Date of Birth .... Time of Birth .... Weight ....

Most Resemblance .... I Hope The Baby Gets Moms ....

I Hope The Baby Gets Dads ....

Happy Memories

Happy Memories

Guest Name

Address and Email

....

....

....

....

Best Advice for Parents

....

....

....

Special Message to Baby

....

....

....

My Predictions

Date of Birth .... Time of Birth........................ Weight........................

Most Resemblance .... I Hope The Baby Gets Moms ....

I Hope The Baby Gets Dads ....

Guest Name

....

Address and Email

....

....

....

Best Advice for Parents

....

....

....

Special Message to Baby

....

....

....

My Predictions

Date of Birth .... Time of Birth .... Weight ....

Most Resemblance .... I Hope The Baby Gets Moms ....

I Hope The Baby Gets Dads ....

Guest Name

Address and Email

....

....

Best Advice for Parents

....

....

....

Special Message to Baby

....

....

....

My Predictions

Date of Birth _____ Time of Birth_____ Weight_____

Most Resemblance _____ I Hope The Baby Gets Moms _____

I Hope The Baby Gets Dads _____

Guest Name

Address and Email

....

....

....

....

Best Advice for Parents

....

....

....

Special Message to Baby

....

....

....

My Predictions

Date of Birth .... Time of Birth........................ Weight........................

Most Resemblance .... I Hope The Baby Gets Moms ....

I Hope The Baby Gets Dads ....

Guest Name

Address and Email

....

....

....

Best Advice for Parents

....

....

....

Special Message to Baby

....

....

....

My Predictions

Date of Birth _____ Time of Birth _____ Weight _____

Most Resemblance _____ I Hope The Baby Gets Moms _____

I Hope The Baby Gets Dads _____

Guest Name

Address and Email

....

....

....

....

Best Advice for Parents

....

....

....

Special Message to Baby

....

....

....

My Predictions

Date of Birth .... Time of Birth .... Weight ....

Most Resemblance .... I Hope The Baby Gets Moms ....

I Hope The Baby Gets Dads ....

Happy Memories

Happy Memories

Gift Log

Gift	Gifted By	Thank you note sent?

Gift Log

Gift	Gifted By	Thank you note sent?

Gift Log

Gift	Gifted By	Thank you note sent?
....	....	....
....	....	....
....	....	....
....	....	....
....	....	....
....	....	....
....	....	....
....	....	....
....	....	....
....	....	....
....	....	....
....	....	....
....	....	....
....	....	....
....	....	....

Gift Log

Gift	Gifted By	Thank you note sent?

Gift Log

Gift	Gifted By	Thank you note sent?

Gift Log

Gift	Gifted By	Thank you note sent?

Gift Log

Gift	Gifted By	Thank you note sent?
....	....	....
....	....	....
....	....	....
....	....	....
....	....	....
....	....	....
....	....	....
....	....	....
....	....	....
....	....	....
....	....	....
....	....	....
....	....	....
....	....	....

Baby Shower Guest Book

Made in the USA
Monee, IL
14 August 2021

75668286R20057